THE DON'T LAUGH CHALLENGE PRESENTS:

THE FARTING EASTER BUNNY

MW01137446

A Fart-Warming Easter Story: A Lactose Intolerant Bunny Brings the Gift of Love, Laughter, and Farts to Easter Sunday

Scan this barcode using your phone camera to access the fart noises for Farting Easter Bunny!

Whenever you see the GREEN EGG at the end of a page, press the fart button on the website that corresponds to the page you are on.

https://www.dontlaughchallenge.com/

RULES

THE DON'T LAUGH CHALLENGE®
FARTING EASTER BUNNY

1. Don't laugh. If you do, you get a point.

2. Don't smile. If you do, you get a point.

3. Farting is Fine. If you do, you can deduct a point from your score.

4. Tally up the points and whoever has the fewest at the end of the book wins the highly coveted title of FART MASTER!

5. Special Tie Breaker below.

In the event of a tie, there is a special bonus Tie Breaker fart button on the website that will determine who is truly the strongest willed among you all. As you read the book you may be tempted to laugh, but in order to win the game, you must do your best to keep a straight face. Farting is not only allowed but encouraged, especially in front of your parents. Everyone knows that parents love your fascination with flatulence, also known as BIG OLE FARTS.

Enjoy the game and book!

J. Cox

Today is a day filled with hunting and cheers,
And eggs and searching, and really big ears.
A bunny is coming to hide many eggs,
But something is coming from behind his hind legs!

There's no need to worry, this story isn't scary.
It's just that the Easter Bunny can't process dairy.
Some can eat ice cream, while others can't -
It's known as being lactose intoler-ant.

Now, you may not know what this means, so I will explain.
If the Easter Bunny eats dairy, then his stomach feels pain,
It grumbles and growls with almost no end!
For the rest of the day, the Easter Bunny breaks wind.
I know some will laugh, but it's not really that funny...
Just imagine what it's like for the poor Easter Bunny!

The gas he expels pushes him into the sky,
Now his regular hop gets three times as high!
Oh, and it's stank! Oh, and it's stink!
It's honestly much worse than you may think.
All of his eggs, every single one, becomes rotten,
And his tail turns green! Yes, the one made of cotton.

8

Now, as some would guess this would mess up his day,
So he stays away from dairy, at least on Easter anyway.
Without knowing, his friend Jenny brought him some quiche,
But she had no clue what she was about to unleash!

"*Thank you, Jenny! These are amazing and delicious,*
But this taste isn't familiar... it's kind of suspicious."

When suddenly, his knees hit the ground,
And his and her ears heard a thunderous sound!

"*It's mainly milk and cheese! Aren't they great?*"

The Easter Bunny's eyes got really big as he thought
of his fate.

When all of a sudden, there's a really big boom,
With a stench so great, it clears the whole room!

"Easter Bunny, what was that?! You just farted?!"

"Jenny, do you have any idea what you've just started?"

"No, Easter Bunny. I had no idea, not one.
But whatever it is, it sure won't be fun."

"What will I do? I have to hide eggs soon.
Your kids plan on hunting eggs this afternoon!"

"My eggs, Jenny! Every one of them, they're all bad!
They smell like garbage mixed with poo, mixed with sad.
I'm scared, Jenny. I don't know what I am going to do.
Kids want eggs, but not ones that smell like poo!
What if I ruin Easter and all those to come,
What if the kids now think that Easter is dumb?!"

13

"Easter Bunny, don't worry about a thing, it's okay!
You're not the only reason kids celebrate Easter Day!
It's really about Jesus and what he has done.
Finding and coloring eggs just adds to the fun!"

"But it is too late to cancel, or come up with a plan.
You will just have to hide them the best that you can.
Bunny, these kids are hunters, they will not tire."

"Don't worry, Jenny! With the force of these farts,
I jump way higher!"

"So, are you gonna hide them in trees?
In the branches with the leaves, and the bees?"

"Yes! I'll put them way, way up high!
On clouds, and on planes, in the sky!"

"But Easter Bunny, don't you think that's too tough?"

"You've smelt these eggs, Jenny! I'm not sure it's enough!"

16

So, he jumps into the trees,
And hides eggs on it's leaves.
Hiding his eggs the best that he could,
He even painted some, so they'd look like wood!

He looks and he finds an enormous beehive -
"This is such a great spot, in here I'll put five!"

But the bees were not happy, no not one bit.
They were so upset, they had a big buzzing fit!
So, they buzzed and they buzzed, and they let out a shout!

"Your eggs are way too smelly! Please, take them out!" 19

So, he grabs all his eggs and he jumps to the sky,
With a powerful fart, he goes three times as high!
He lands on a cloud that is so fluffy and white,
And all of the clouds were a delight to his sight.

But as soon as his eggs touch the cloud,
Easter Bunny hears something very loud.
The cloud begins to rumble, and even turn green,
The clouds have turned into a farting machine!

Easter Bunny gasps at the gas that's brewing insight,

"I guess I should go put some on a plane that's inflight."

And he leaps up again, faster than a dart,

And he's even faster when he uses his fart!

He lands on a plane and puts eggs on its wings,
While the people inside yell, "What are those things?!"
Easter Bunny says, "They're my eggs. I must hide them now!"

"Do you have to hide them here? I mean holy cow!"

"They're so smelly, it's a horrible scent!
And because this is a plane, I can't open the vent!
So, if you would sir, please take them away."

Easter Bunny says, "Sorry, it's too loud out here.
Have a good day!"

He leaps from the plane, and heads towards the ground,
Hoping that not one of his eggs would be found.
But what he sees while he is falling,
Could only be explained as extremely appalling!

All of the kids, yes, every single one,
They were all playing, and yes, having fun!
They were up in the trees,
Finding eggs on their leaves.

Some crafty kids tied themselves to a kite,
And grabbed the eggs from the clouds,
And even the plane inflight!

"This doesn't make sense, what are they doing?
They should be giving up, not laughing and ewwing!"

So, he jumps over to see why the kids are still playing,

"How can they even breathe near the eggs I've been laying?"

"Kids, how are you having so much fun?
I was sure once you got one whiff, you'd surely be done!"

"But Mr. Easter Bunny, these eggs are great!
With this strong smell, we can tell what you've ate!"

Easter Bunny just stood there, in a state of shock.
After hearing the joyful laughter, he's unable to talk.
"So, Mr. Bunny, your eggs, have we found them all?"
Easter Bunny was still so surprised, he couldn't recall.

"I guess you did, kids! You have done very well,
But how did you even breathe near these eggs smell?"

"Well honestly Mr. Bunny, the smell is not that bad,
If you think those farts are nasty, you should meet
my dad!"

So, Easter Bunny stood there in deep thought -
"These kids were not upset, no they were not,
I guess it doesn't matter if my eggs smell like farts,
What really matters is kids have Christ in their hearts."

Made in the USA
Columbia, SC
01 April 2021

35539261R00020